ISLINGTO
and CLERKENWELL

A Portrait in Old Picture Postcards

by

Jim Connell and Dick Whetstone

S. B. Publications
1991

CONTENTS

CONTENTS

Cover illustration: Imperial Garage, Ingleby Road, 1910.

Nine houses were built in Ingleby Road in 1869. At first the only business premises were a physician, a dressmaker and a clog-maker. Then, in 1910, William Price opened his motorcycle garage, which later became H. Dwight & Son, motor engineers.

INTRODUCTION

The London Borough of Islington is an amalgamation of two former Metropolitan Boroughs, Finsbury and Islington. Our first book of postcards represented only the older Islington, the Parish of St. Mary; this second book includes also some pictures of Clerkenwell. Islington was already established by the time of the Norman Conquest, though only in a small way, for the Domesday Book shows 27 householders living in "Iseldone" and another nine in "Tolentone" (the Hornsey Road area). The name of Clerkenwell dates from the 12th century when the Ancient Company of Parish Clerks first performed miracle and mystery plays near a well (it is still there in Farringdon Lane, and now a tourist attraction) which thus came to be named Clerks' Well. A nunnery dedicated to St. Mary was founded about 1100 where St. James' Church is now, and the Priory of St. John of Jerusalem was built in Clerkenwell in the 12th century. Both were suppressed by Henry VIII.

During the 16th and 17th centuries Islington, separated from London by fields and farmland, became a rural retreat from the cares of high office for nobles and courtiers from the courts of Henry VIII and Elizabeth, who set up second homes here. In the 17th and 18th centuries both Finsbury and Islington attracted many visitors to the spas, tea-gardens and other entertainments.

Finsbury became urbanized earlier than Islington. In 1800 the population of Clerkenwell and Finsbury was 23,000, whereas Islington had a mere 10,000 inhabitants, and over nine-tenths of its area was still farmland. As the 19th century advanced Finsbury became entirely built up, and it became one of the inner, rather than the outer, suburbs of London. By the end of the 18th century, a small amount of upper middle class housing – Highbury Place and Terrace, and Canonbury Place – had been built in Islington, to be followed in the early 19th century by the impressive squares and terraces in Barnsbury and Canonbury. But it was not until the second half of the century that the population rose rapidly to 334,991 in 1901, and the rate of house-building was such that the only open land left was the 25-acre space of Highbury Fields, rescued from the developers in 1885.

The photographs in this book date mainly from the first decade of the 20th century. Motor-buses had started running in 1906 and electric trams in 1908, but much of the transport was still horsedrawn, and the roads look quiet and uncluttered, except for Chapel Market which was as crowded then as it is today. The dates ascribed to the various pictures are mainly the result of educated guesswork, using internal clues in the photographs, and are probably correct to within five years.

Jim Connell
August 1991

ST. JOHN'S GATE

Probably the oldest building in Islington, this gate was built by Prior Thomas Docwra in 1504 as the south entrance to the Priory of St. John of Jerusalem. It was the second priory on the site, the first one having been destroyed by Wat Tyler in the Peasants' Revolt in 1381. Henry VIII dissolved the priory in 1540 and much of the stonework was dismantled to be used to build Somerset House. This gate was spared and had subsequent use as a printer's office, a watch house, even a tavern until 1873 when it once again became the headquarters of the Most Venerable Order of St. John of Jerusalem; it now houses the Order's museum and library.

186 LONDON. – St. John's Gate, Clerkenwel. – LL

NORTHAMPTON INSTITUTE, c. 1920

On this site in St. John Street once stood the manor house of Clerkenwell Manor, owned by the Northampton family. It was later used successively as a private asylum, a girls' school and the Manor House Boys' School until 1898 when the Northampton Institute in this photograph was opened by the Marquess of Northampton. The building was much extended in 1966 and changed its name to The City University.

MYDDELTON SQUARE, c. 1910

Myddelton Square was built in 1827 (the same year as St. Mark's Church in the centre of the square), and was named after Sir Hugh Myddelton, the man who created the New River to bring pure drinking water to London. The church suffered some damage during the war, and received a new east window in 1962.

MYDDELTON SQUARE, c. 1910

Lord Brockway, who died in 1988 aged 99, a pioneer member of the Labour party, as Fenner Brockway, M.P. for Eton and Slough 1950–64, lived as a young man at 60 Myddelton Square.

METROPOLITAN WATER BOARD OFFICES, 1920

Built in 1920 on the site of the offices of the New River Company, one of the eight water companies from which the MWB was formed. The site of the Round Pond, which was made in 1613 to receive the water from Amwell, is behind the new offices. Rosebery Avenue was built in 1889–93, bridging the Fleet Valley, by the new London County Council, and opened in 1895 by the Council's first chairman, Lord Rosebery.

AMWELL STREET, c. 1910

Behind the viewpoint of this photograph, on the right, is the site of the Round Pond, the reservoir of the New River, constructed in 1613. In 1709 a reservoir was built on higher ground, known as the High Pond, and it still exists, behind the trees on the right in the far distance. It was popular with local anglers until it was covered over in 1856 as a sanitary measure. Houses were built round the reservoir in the 1820s, and are now named Claremont Square. Charles Frederick Brust had the bakery shop on the corner of River Street for over thirty years. This quiet scene, with no traffic except a pony-trap and Brust's delivery van parked outside the shop, contrasts with present-day "rat-run" problems.

MYDDELTON STREET, 1915

Myddelton Street dates back from 1813–14. In the centre, on the corner of Garnault Place and Myddelton Street, is Myddelton House, built in 1862, the office of the Clerkenwell News, and later the Daily Chronicle. Charles Henry Baker, fancy draper, took over the premises about 1900. On the right is a beer house which later became the Nettlefolds pub, and on the extreme left, just visible, the Finsbury Town Hall, built in 1895.

ELECTRIC CAR, ST. JOHN STREET, 1906–7

The Kingsway subway opened as far as Aldwych in 1908, with a service of single-decker trams to the Angel. There is still a horse-drawn bus running, but within a year of this photograph it would have been replaced by a motor-bus. The Angel Inn was re-modelled with its new dome in 1899†, and the ornamental gas-lamp on the right is on the Old Red Lion. John Henry Ross boldly advertises his "Cheap Stationery" at No. 441, next door to Joseph Emanuel the fruiterer; nor is there any doubt about the location of the Express Dairy with its name in enormous letters mounted high on the building.

† There is more about the Angel Inn in the first volume of Islington postcards.

DUNCAN TERRACE, c. 1910

A number of terraces built along the bank of the New River in the late 18th century were numbered throughout as one and named Duncan Terrace in 1890. Public gardens have been laid out along where the river once flowed. (Terraces on the opposite bank were similarly unified in 1864 as Colebrooke Row.) The Roman Catholic Church of St. John the Evangelist was built in 1843. Bruce Kent was the priest in the years 1980–84.

UPPER STREET, c. 1920

On the left, by the corner of Liverpool Road, at No. 1 Upper Street, is William Smith the pawnbroker, established 1760, but in these premises from the 1840s. The shop was demolished a few years ago, and rebuilt in its orginal form, to be the Islington office of the Halifax Building Society. The Home & Colonial, one of eight branches in Islington, opened in the late 19th century until about 1930. In recent memory it was Stones, television and radio dealer, but is now demolished.

ISLINGTON CENTRAL MISSION, c. 1910

The chapel on the left, on the corner of Barford Street, was the Wesleyan chapel built in 1849 to replace a former one which was burnt out, and was known at this time as Islington Central Mission Church. It was closed and was demolished in 1929, when it amalgamated with Drayton Park Mission and built the Islington Central Hall in Drayton Park. Young men and women of the Mission formed a band in 1897 to accompany services in pubs and lodging houses, and to spread the Gospel at open-air gatherings. Here they are apparently assembled for a day in the country.

CHAPEL STREET, ISLINGTON, N.

CHAPEL STREET, 1909

Chapel Street (renamed Chapel Market in 1936) started being built in 1790 as a residential street. It was officially designated a market in 1879, though it had been used by stallholders for years before that, to the annoyance of the genteel residents. The shop on the extreme left, the first shop at the Liverpool Road end of the Market, was Henry Kennett, a grocer, followed by butcher William Shelbourn, and John Sainsbury, who first opened his provision shop here in 1880. Note the flower-girls in the foreground.

CHAPEL STREET, 1926

The "Bargain Corner" is at 52 Chapel Market, on the corner of a narrow alley leading to Emmen's Buildings behind the shops, and was owned by boot and shoe dealer Harris Paskin.

ISLINGTON HIGH STREET, c. 1920

Myddelton Buildings on the left were built by the Improved Industrial Dwellings Company in 1882. They were demolished in 1968 but the entrance arch survived for a few years. The entrance to the Grand Theatre (1860–1962) lies beyond the White Swan pub. Past the four-storeyed White Lion on the left is the tower of the Angel Cinema, built in 1912 and closed in 1973, and the Angel Inn. The London Joint City & Midland Bank took over a former grocer with a sideline as a post office savings bank about 1920, and stayed there, as the Midland Bank, until 1990 when it moved up the street to the deserted White Lion.

UPPER STREET, c. 1920

A private house at No. 45 was converted into a pub in 1831, named the Star and Garter. It was renamed the Champion in 1973 to honour its landlord, Len Harvey, a former boxer who had held the British light-heavy and heavyweight titles. In 1983 it took the new name of the Passage. The three shops next to the pub belonged to William Huntsman, an ironmongers, a brushmaker, and a pottery and glass shop. Beyond that were the fancy draper's and the hosier's of John Andrew Haslop. Parked outside the Star & Garter is a "Bullnose" Morris Cowley, in production 1919–1926.

ISLINGTON GREEN, c. 1920

Once a bit of spare ground at the junction of two roads, and used as a rubbish tip, the Green was given to the people of Islington by the Marquess of Northampton in 1777. The statue of Sir Hugh Myddelton, who created the New River in 1613 to bring pure drinking water to London, was erected in 1862 where previously had stood the watch house, Islington's first police station.

COLLINS MUSIC HALL, c. 1910

A small pub on Islington Green, the Lansdowne Tavern, opened a singing room in 1790 for the entertainment of its customers. In 1862 the room was enlarged as the Lansdowne Music Hall, but had little success until Sam Collins, an entertainer with experience in management, bought it in 1863 and gave it his name. It was rebuilt, taking in the shop next door, in 1897. The end came in 1958 when a fire which spread from Andersons' woodyard in Essex Road caused so much damage that it never re-opened. George Robey, Charlie Chaplin, Tommy Trinder, Norman Wisdom and Gracie Fields are some of the great names who have appeared here.

ST. PETER'S STREET, 1907

Thomas Alva Edison invented the phonograph which played a wax cylinder in 1877; Alexander Graham Bell improved it in 1885, and in 1904 the disc-type gramophone record was introduced. William Hanneman, who ran a barber-shop in St. Peter's Street from c. 1903 to 1912, supplemented his income from haircuts and shaves by venturing into a sideline of this modern technology.

ISLINGTON CHAPEL, UPPER STREET

Islington Chapel was first built in Gaskin Street (named Church Street until 1937) in 1789–93. A new chapel was built in 1814 on this site, but when Upper Street was widened in 1886 a new larger chapel was built. In 1974 it united with Claremont Chapel and in 1979 the building was sold, and all activities were transferred to the Islington-Claremont United Reform Church in White Lion Street.

CROSS STREET, c. 1905

The Confectioner's shop soon afterwards became an ostrich feather merchant; next door is Edwin Honey the tobacconist, and W.R. Watts developed into Watts, Cornish & Company, leather merchants. Past the end of Halton Road is the chapel built in 1852 by Baptists who had been using an old Calvinist chapel built in Providence Place (Behind the Screen-on-the-Green cinema) in 1820. The Cross Street chapel was bombed during the war and rebuilt in 1957.

WELCOME TO THE DUKE OF FIFE, 1905

On the 15th July 1905 a huge crowd waited to see the Duke of Fife, Lord Lieutenant of the County of London, on his way to Highbury Fields to unveil the War Memorial to Islington men who died in the South African War. T.R. Roberts opened his drapery at 222 Upper Street in 1862, and gradually took over the neighbouring shops until by 1918 he owned the complete stretch from No. 208 to No. 225, except for one.

WELCOME TO THE DUKE OF FIFE, 1905

The one business which T.R. Roberts could not buy out was the Islington branch of the National Provincial Bank at No. 218, which opened in 1870. Roberts closed in 1953, having suffered severe bomb damage in 1941, but the bank is still there as the National Westminster, having been rebuilt on a larger scale (taking in No. 219) in 1951–52.

COMPTON TERRACE, c. 1910

Union Chapel was built in open fields in 1806, with a pair of houses on each side. More houses were added until the terrace was completed in 1831. It then extended as far as St. Paul's Road, across the grassy middle of the traffic roundabout, the end house facing the Cock Tavern.

COMPTON TERRACE, c. 1920

On the 27th June 1944 a flying bomb fell on Highbury Corner, and the end eleven houses of Compton Terrace, those in the foreground of this picture, were destroyed.

CANONBURY PLACE, c. 1910

The building behind the trees is the back of the east range of Canonbury House. Part of this was demolished and new houses built by John Dawes in the late 18th century. Nos. 6 and 7 of these new houses were converted in 1878 by the Girls' Public Day School Trust into Highbury and Islington High School, offering a broad education with preparation for the Oxford and Cambridge Schools Board examinations. In 1908 it was recognised as efficient by the Board of Education, one of only five secondary schools in Islington to be so approved. It closed in 1911.

COMPTON ROAD, c. 1910

Compton Road was built about 1850, from Canonbury Square to St. Paul's Road, which can be seen in the distance. Originally named as Downing Terrace, Northampton Terrace and St. George's Villas, it was renumbered in 1868, and the old names were abolished in favour of the present one.

CANONBURY PARK SOUTH, c. 1910

This was known as Crescent Road when groups of houses individually named as Priory Villas, Hope Villas, Alwyne Cottages and Chester Villas were built in the 1840s. In 1865 it was given its present name and the houses were renumbered. This view is from the corner of Willowbridge Road.

CANONBURY PARK SOUTH, c. 1900

This is a view from the St. Paul's Road end of Canonbury Park South.

NEW RIVER, DOUGLAS ROAD, c. 1910

The river was there over 200 years before the road. Sir Hugh Myddelton constructed the New River from Amwell in Hertfordshire, running through Islington and Finsbury to end at the New River Head in Amwell Street in 1613. Douglas Road dates from about 1850.

BENWELL ROAD, c. 1910

Benwell Road was built between 1864 and 1870. The Montague Arms, on the corner of Bryantwood Road, dates from the early 1870s.

ELFORT ROAD, c. 1905

Elfort Road, an "infill" street of small working-class houses, was built during the 1870s and 1880s. This view is from Aubert Park; at the far end the street turns left into Drayton Park. Note the tin bath hanging outside the shop on the right. No bathrooms in these houses in those days – you put the bath in front of the kitchen fire, and filled it with water heated in pans and kettles.

BATTLEDEAN ROAD, c. 1910

Battledean Road and nearby Framfield Road (from where this photograph is taken), an estate of small middle-class houses, were built in the 1890s in a wedge-shaped gap between the railway cutting and Highbury Terrace Mews.

CALABRIA ROAD, c. 1910

One of several small residential streets built about 1890 behind Corsica Street. Corsica Street was originally Highbury Mews, a service road to Highbury Place. The streets in this area were named after Roman provinces because it was believed (erroneously, according to moden archaeologists) that the Roman army had a summer camp on Highbury Hill.

CALABRIA ROAD, c. 1910

This is a view of Calabria Road from where it crosses Corsica Street, showing its zigzag course; it has four sharp bends in its meandering length.

LIBERIA ROAD, c. 1910

Liberia Road runs from Calabria Road to Fergus Road which can be seen in the distance.

BAALBEC ROAD, c. 1910

Another road in the "Roman" estate, showing Highbury Grove at the end of the street.

BAPTIST CHURCH, HIGHBURY HILL, c. 1905

A chapel was built on Highbury Hill in 1862, on the corner of Aubert Park, but was disused by 1864. The church in this photograph was built on the same site in 1871. It was demolished in 1959 and a block of flats named Tawney Court was built in its place.

AUBERT PARK, c. 1905

Aubert Park started out in 1825 as College Road when it was the access road to the newly-built St. John's College of Divinity. After being developed as a residential road it was named in 1877 after Lt-Col. Alexander Aubert, commanding officer of the Loyal Islington Volunteers, and a one-time resident of Highbury Hill. The college leased its sports ground to Woolwich Arsenal Football Club in 1913. After a disastrous fire in 1946 the college was demolished and Aubert Court was built on the site. Arsenal Football Club is, of course, still there.

HAMILTON PARK, c. 1905

Hamilton Road (renamed Park in 1938) was built in the 1850s as a series of residential terraces. Only the end nearest Highbury Park (the viewpoint of this photograph) had any business occupation. On the left is a beer and wine dealer, and Stainton's sign is at the entrance to a large yard containing stables and also the Highbury Post Sorting Office.

ELPHINSTONE STREET, c. 1905

Built in 1881–82 and named after 18th century Islington resident James Elphinstone, uncle of Islington's vicar, Dr. Strahan, and friend of Dr. Johnson.

KELROSS ROAD, c. 1910

Kelross Road developed from Newington Lane, an 18th century footpath across the fields to Green Lanes; Collins Road, formerly Paradise Road, is the other end of the old lane. In 1920 a temporary Roman Catholic chapel was built in Kelross Road, dedicated to St. Joan of Arc. (Joan was canonized in 1920, so this was probably the first church dedicated to her.) A new church was built in 1961–62 in Highbury Park, on the site of a former Carmelite nunnery, and the chapel became a church hall.

NORTHOLME ROAD, c.1910

It takes its name from North Holm, the name of an estate on which this, Sotheby and Aberdeen Road were built in the early 1890s. ("Holm" is a Middle English term for flat low-lying ground.)

HIGHBURY PARK BROADWAY, c. 1910

Highbury Park Broadway, an impressive parade of shops, was built in 1895 when Highbury Park was widened at this point. The Ten Per Cent Wine Company's shop on the corner of Northolme Road is No. 1 The Broadway.

SOTHEBY ROAD, c. 1910

Built on the North Holm, Sotheby Road was first occupied in 1892.

HIGHBURY NEW PARK, c. 1910

Henry Rydon, a property developer, laid out Highbury New Park in 1853. Beresford Terrace, which dates from about 1860, is on the right.

ST. AUGUSTINE'S CHURCH, c. 1920

In 1864 Henry Rydon built a temporary corrugated-iron church, seating 850, in Highbury New Park. It was replaced in 1869–70 by this church of brick with stone dressings. Between the church and Highbury Quadrant School is a footpath leading to Petherton Road

GROSVENOR ROAD, c. 1910

Known as Grosvenor Avenue since 1938 this road was built up in 1870–71. In the distance is the spire of Park Church which was built by Scotch Congregationalists in 1861. It was bombed in 1940 and only the facade remained until 1952. A block of flats named Parkchurch House was built on the site in 1955. On the left is the corner of Wallace Road where Canonbury Station stands.

CANONBURY STATION, c. 1905

This station was built in Wallace Road in 1870 by the North London Railway and replaced a station on Newington Green Road which had been built twelve years earlier. The houses straight ahead are in Grosvenor Avenue.

BALFOUR ROAD, c. 1910

A road which runs along three sides of a rectangle, starting and finishing on Highbury New Park, intersected by Stradbroke Road. Both roads date from 1875–76.

THE ROYAL OAK, GREEN LANES, c. 1910

There has been a Royal Oak (and a Pegasus, just up the road) on Green Lanes since at least 1848. Leconfield Road dates from the 1870s.

PICKFORD'S DELIVERY VAN, c. 1910

Pickford & Company Ltd., general carriers and contractors to the North Western Railway, had a furniture repository at 114 Blackstock Road, and their office and commercial removals office is still there.

BLACKSTOCK ROAD, c. 1930

It is difficult to imagine that this was once known as Blackstock Lane, a narrow way bordered by hedges and wild flowers. There were no buildings there in 1840, but two or three houses had appeared by 1850. It was officially named as Blackstock Road in 1876.

SEVEN SISTERS ROAD, 1935–37

This view is taken from the corner of Station Road looking east towards Manor House; St. Thomas's Road is on the right. The dome of Alexandra Buildings, on the corner of Blackstock Road, can just be seen, and beyond it the spire of the Wesleyan Church. The tram is a "Feltham", a type which was introduced in 1931, but not fitted with the plough (underground contact) until the late 1930s. In 1951 the Felthams were sold to Leeds Corporation where they remained in service until 1959.

TRAM TERMINUS, FINSBURY PARK, c. 1920

A similar view to that of the previous card, from the corner of Stroud Green Road. The spire in the distance is that of the Wesleyan Church on the corner of Wilberforce Road, built in 1875. It was demolished in 1959 and a petrol station is now on the site.

FINSBURY GATE, SEVEN SISTERS ROAD, 1904–05

The North Metropolitan Tramways Company started electrification north of Finsbury Park in July 1904 on the overhead system, the earliest electric service north of the Thames. The newspaper placard refers to the Russo-Japanese War, 1904–5.

THE ASTORIA, SEVEN SISTERS ROAD, c. 1937

Islington has some notable examples of interior design like the Elizabethan ceilings of Canonbury Tower, the Jacobean carving of the Oak Room of the Metropolitan Water Board, and the flying angel lamp-brackets of the old Finsbury Town Hall, but none was arrayed like the Astoria Cinema, built in 1930, with a seating capacity of over 3,000. Subtle lighting effects made the ceiling look like open sky and the proscenium arch was surrounded by the representation of an Andalucian village. In 1971 it closed as a cinema and re-opened as the Rainbow Theatre with a series of pop concerts. It is now a Grade II listed building, and is owned by the church group New Living Ministries. On the left is the Clarence pub, now named Sir George Robey in memory of the self-styled Prime Minister of Mirth who often appeared at the nearby Finsbury Park Empire.

96, SEVEN SISTERS ROAD, c. 1910

Emerton & Sons dairies sold out to Premier Dairies Ltd. about 1920.

PECK'S, 10–16 ESSEX ROAD, c. 1920

Samuel Peck, at first, had only Nos. 10, 12 and 14. He had to wait for the Grand Furnishing Company to move out before he could extend to the whole block located between St. Peter's Street and Elliott's Place, and put his name in big letters on the wall to be seen by all travelling along Essex Road.

CORONET CINEMA, ESSEX ROAD, c. 1915

The Northern District Post Office was built in 1855 on the corner of Packington Street. It moved in 1905 to the newly-built office in Upper Street. In 1911 the old Essex Road building was converted to the Coronet Cinema. In 1931 it was acquired by the Blue Hall Cinema at the Royal Agricultural Hall, and continued to show films until 1941 as the Blue Hall Annexe. It is now named Merchants Hall, the home of William Bedford Antiques. To the right of the cinema is the Old Queen's Head; there has been a pub on this site since the days of the first Queen Elizabeth.

THE THREE BREWERS, ESSEX ROAD, c. 1905

This pub has successfully slaked Islington thirsts under the name of The Three Brewers since about 1830, but in the last few years it has had an identity crisis, renamed as The Jersey, then the Speculator, and now Leopold Bloom's. Next to the pub is Alfred Bond, linen draper. The horse on the right is striving to get a run at the hill up Canonbury Road. The trams used to put on an extra horse at this point.

ESSEX ROAD, 1905

This view looks east from River Place. On the corner of Canonbury Road is the advertisement of Charles Venables & Company, piano makers of 187 and 189 Essex Road and 2 and 4 Canonbury Road. The Essex Road tube station, half-hidden behind the tree, was opened in 1904 by the Great Northern & City Railway. On the right are the ornamental lamps of The Three Brewers. St. Matthew's Church, built on the corner of Canonbury Street in 1851, was covered with a luxuriant growth of ivy, and was popularly called the "Ivy Church"; it suffered damage in the war and was demolished when Eric Fletcher Court was built in 1958.

ESSEX ROAD, c. 1900

This stretch of Essex Road, from Northampton Street on the left to Canonbury Street on the right, was built in the 1820s as Northampton Terrace. There are many examples in Islington of terraces of private houses converted to commercial use by the building of single-storey shops on the front gardens, a type of development which is very obvious in this photograph. The first two shops, dining rooms and a hairdresser, were established in the 19th century, but changed about 1930 to a wholesale grocer; the cycle shop was opened in 1890 and so remained, under various owners, until 1923. The Wincycle Trading Company of Saffron Hill distributed its bicycles through many retail outlets in London.

ESSEX ROAD, c. 1905

The row of houses named Scott's Place was built in 1804 from New North Road (then King Street) to Queensbury Street (which was then named Queen Street and came north as far as Essex Road). The houses were converted into shops by building on the front gardens, and the Golden Fleece dates from this time. Bentham Court (named for Ethel Bentham, a former Member of Parliament for Islington) was built on partially bomb-damaged property across Queensbury Road in 1946–49, and a new row of shops was built on Essex Road, standing behind a narrow service road. The Golden Fleece would have been in front of Nos. 208–210.

THE GOLDEN FLEECE, ESSEX ROAD, c. 1910

Beer delivery day at the Golden Fleece. Many pubs advertised their presences with large ornate lamps outside the building; these on the Golden Fleece must be some of the biggest.

ESSEX ROAD, c. 1910

Behind the trees on the right lies Annett's Crescent, named after Thomas Annett, the developer of the property, built about 1820, between Rotherfield and Halliford Streets. The villas on the left were replaced in 1958 by Eric Fletcher Court, named after a former Islington Member of Parliament.

ROTHERFIELD STREET, 1905

A view from Ecclesbourne Road towards St. Matthew's Church on Essex Road. The light-coloured building at the end of the row is the end house of Annett's Crescent, and next to it is the Duke of Clarence pub, dating from about 1860.

ESSEX ROAD, 1910

The Northampton Arms, popularly known as "The Old Red House", stood on the corner of Ashby Grove, a street of large semi-detached villas built about 1850. Behind the railings on the left Sickert Court (named after artist Walter Sickert who had a studio here) was built in 1948. Ashby Road (it was not named "Grove" until 1938) and the pub have disappeared under the Marquess estate, built 1973–77.

CROWLAND TERRACE, c. 1905

A short street of only eight houses, Crowland Terrace was built in 1865 between Northchurch and Englefield Roads.

ESSEX ROAD, c. 1910

Englefield Road, on the right, dates from 1860. The bank on the corner was the London & Provincial, later the National Westminster. The electric tram is just passing the end of Clephane Road, built in 1850, and named after Margaret Clephane, wife of the Marquess of Northampton. Clephane Road and its large houses have been absorbed by the Marquess estate.

MARQUESS ROAD, c. 1905

Marquess Road today is but a fraction of the street of fine houses built in 1853 from Canonbury Grove to St. Paul's Church. Arran Walk, Oronsay Walk and Scarba Walk of the Marquess estate follow the line of the original road. The church was built in 1826–28 on the corner of St. Paul's and Essex Roads.

ST. PHILIP'S CHURCH, LINTON STREET, c. 1905

St. Philip's was built in 1855. The following year a church school was built behind the church (you can see the school bell on the roof in this photograph); it was taken over by the School Board of London from 1901 to 1911, and then became a church hall. The church was closed in 1953 and has been demolished, and the vicarage to the right of the church has been converted into flats.

ST. PAUL'S ROAD, C. 1910

The building of terraces of middle-class houses along an ancient track named Hopping Lane started in 1850. The name St. Paul's Road was officially adopted in 1862. Compton Road on the right dates from the same period. The Alwyne Castle pub (Alwyne is a family name of the Marquess of Northampton) is visible beyond the trees. It was bombed during the war, and carried on business in a pre-fab until it was rebuilt in its present form in 1967.

GRANGE ROAD, c. 1910

We know this street as Grange Grove, the name it was given in 1938. It was built in 1867 between St. Paul's Road and Canonbury Place.

ST. PAUL'S CHURCH, c. 1905

St. Paul's was built in 1826–28 at the corner of St. Paul's and Essex Roads, one of three new churches to accommodate the growing population of Islington. (The other two were St. John's, Upper Holloway and Holy Trinity, Cloudesley Square.)

MILDMAY GROVE, c. 1910

These terraces were built in the 1870s on each side of the North London Railway, from King Henry's Walk to Newington Green Road, and were named as North Grove and South Grove, each one divided into East and West. The present name was adopted in 1877. The photograph shows the houses on what was South Grove West, that is the stretch from Mildmay Park to Newington Green Road. F.J. Bunker the dairyman marked his name indelibly on the flank wall of the house, but by the time this photograph was taken the business was being run by Ernest Alexander Bunker. Five of the houses here were let out in rooms in 1910.

MILDMAY PARK FOOTBALL CLUB, 1912

We have been unable to discover any facts about the Mildmay Park Football Club, despite lengthy searches of the sports reports in several local newspapers of the period, and enquiries of the London Football Association. Perhaps some reader can help?

POET'S ROAD, c. 1910

Poet's Road and Leconfield Road were laid out in 1873; Leconfield was completed by 1877, but Poet's Road was not finished until 1883. It was named for Samuel Rogers, banker and amateur poet (1762–1855) who was offered, and declined, the Poet Laureateship when Wordsworth died in 1850. Rogers lived in a large house on the south-west corner of Newington Green which was demolished in 1883 when Nos. 2 to 10 Ferntower Road were built. An important building in the otherwise residential Poet's Road was the Dalston Synagogue (so named because the congregation had its beginning in Birkbeck Road, Dalston), built in 1885 and demolished in 1967, the site being used for housing.

NEWINGTON GREEN, c. 1920

Newington Green started developing in the 16th century from a clearing in the Forest of Middlesex into a residential area for prosperous Londoners looking for an out-of-town home. The houses and shops nearest the camera were built in the 1880s on the site of a large house and garden where lived the poet Samuel Rogers. The four shops in the middle of the picture, with gabled fronts, now numbered 52 to 55, were built as dwelling houses in 1658, and are probably the oldest houses (except for Canonbury Tower) still standing in Islington. The building in the distance was an 18th century house extended and converted into a factory in 1909, and later became the North London depot of Brook Bond Oxo. The old part of the house was demolished in 1965.

HIGHBURY STATION, c. 1910

This station, replacing a row of shops and incorporating a re-sited Cock Tavern, was built by the North London Railway in 1872 to cope with Highbury's increasing commuter traffic. A flying-bomb on the 27th June 1944 severely damaged both station and pub. The Cock was rebuilt in 1956, and the Post Office was built on the open space in front of the station.

HOLLOWAY ROAD, c. 1920

The building on the right, half-hidden by the tree, was the home and office of estate agent James Wagstaff until 1910 when it became a branch of the London & Provincial Bank, later Barclays. Over its many years from at least the early 19th century the White Swan has also been called the Old Swan and the Old White Swan. The building to its left was the post office; when the station was remodelled to take the Victoria Line in 1968 the post office and the pub were demolished; a new post office was built in the forecourt of the station, but they did not build a new White Swan.

HIGHBURY UNDERGROUND STATION, c. 1910

The Great Northern & City Electric Railway opened this station in 1904 on Holloway Road. It was closed in 1968 when the Victoria Line was constructed, and the railway station across the road was adapted to serve both the old Northern Line and the Victoria line.

HOLLOWAY ROAD, c. 1900

This and the next postcard are the same scene observed from opposite viewpoints. The Coach & Horses pub, dating from the early 19th century, was compulsorily purchased in 1966 to be demolished to make way for the extension to the Polytechnic of North London, but the shops from Slaney Place to Hornsey Road are still there. The large block of flats beyond Hornsey Road are Manhattan Mansions, built in 1894, but recently replaced, together with the pawn shop on the corner, by steel and glass.

HOLLOWAY ROAD, c. 1900

Sidney Stone the butcher, who had his own small abattoir behind the shop, could be said to be well-established for he had three more shops in Holloway Road. In the distance is the North London Polytechnic built in 1896 "to promote the industrial skill, general knowledge, health and well being of young men and women belonging to the poorer classes of Islington". It was extended in 1966, replacing two pubs (the Coach & Horses and the Pied Bull), the Essoldo Cinema and several shops. In 1971 it amalgamated with the North Western Polytechnic, Kentish Town, to be the Polytechnic of North London.

HOLLOWAY ROAD, c. 1935

Edward Beale learned the baker's trade at his uncle John's shop in Oxford Street. In 1829 he set up his own bakery in Popham Street, helped by his nephew William. William Beale opened a shop on Highgate Hill before moving in 1866 to a part of Holloway Road named Pleasant Row, which included an early 19th century pub, the King's Head, which is still there and has retained some highly decorative carved wood panels. Here William Beale built this ornate shop in 1889 on the corner of Tollington Road, including a bakery and shop, restaurant and banqueting hall. He leased the corner shop, for many years to Jones the jeweller, and later to Mayfair Shoes. Sainsburys demolished the complex in 1970 and built a supermarket.

LORAINE MANSIONS, c. 1930

Loraine Mansions were built in Widdenham Road, off Caldedonian Road, in 1904.

1316a. Nag's Head, Holloway.

NAG'S HEAD, HOLLOWAY, c. 1910

An ancient track named Heame Lane, which ran from Holloway Road to the foot of Stroud Green, was extended in 1831 to form a road to Tottenham. It terminated near a group of seven elm trees known locally as the Seven Sisters. The Nag's Head, though not one of the oldest pubs in Holloway Road, dates from the early 19th century. Next to the pub along Seven Sisters Road was a tobacconist, and Richard Samuel Parkes had the next two shops with his name painted high on the wall, matched by butchers Rayner, King & Hardwick further down the road.

YORK ROAD, c. 1910

This photograph was taken from the point where Hungerford and Cliff Roads cross York Way, and looks north towards the Camden Road crossing. The light-coloured building in the middle of the picture, on the left of the road, is the Brecknock Arms, these days known as the Unicorn Tavern.

CUMMING STREET, c. 1910

Cumming Street dates from about 1780 when Henry Penton was developing his housing estate. It originally ran from Pentonville Road to Wynford Road but was cut short in 1951 when the Priory Green estate was built. On the left is the George IV pub, and behind the trees on the right is St. James' Church, built in 1787 and rebuilt in facsimile in 1990 as an office block. Cumming was the name of one of the building contractors.

PENTONVILLE ROAD, c. 1910

This was named the New Road when it was made in 1756, but none of the buildings now on Pentonville Road date from earlier than the mid to late 19th century. Rabbits & Sons were bootmakers, and next door were pawnbrokers G.H. & F.W. Bravington, who later moved into the corner premises shown here as the Victoria Hotel. Next to the pawnbrokers was Blofeld's dining rooms, a fruiterer, and a Lyons' tea-shop.

THE STORES, 53 DONEGAL STREET, c. 1910

Robert Henry Pullen stands proprietorially at the door of his off-licence shop on the corner of Donegal and Rodney Streets.

CALEDONIAN ROAD, c. 1910

This view looks south towards Pentonville Road from the corner of Northdown Street. On the corner is the grocer William Brothers, then the Pocock Brothers, bootmakers, holding their "Great Annual Sale".

CHARLOTTE STREET CHAPEL, c. 1900

This chapel was built by the Wesleyan Methodist Association in Charlotte Street (renamed Carnegie Street in 1938) in 1841. It could seat a congregation of 860, and had a large schoolroom in the basement. In 1857 it was renamed the United Methodist Free Church, and in 1907 became known as the King's Cross Mission. It was destroyed by a land-mine on the 13th April 1941, four months short of its hundredth birthday, and the area was covered with Council flats in the 1950s.

CALEDONIAN ROAD, c. 1905

A company was formed in 1826 to build a road from King's Cross to Holloway Road. It was named Chalk Road (renamed Caledonian Road in 1953) and ran through open fields for most of its length. Terraces built in the 1850s suffered from poor drainage and polluted air, so houses which had been intended for middle-class family residences changed to trades and crafts, and some were multi-occupied by poor families. In a novel published in 1887 Caledonian Road is described thus: "It is doubtful if London can show any thoroughfare of importance more offensive to eye and ear and nostril". This view shows the crossroads with Copenhagen Street, with the Milford Haven pub on the right and the Sutton Arms diagonally opposite. The corn dealer is the Essex Flour & Grain Company.

CALEDONIAN ROAD BATHS, c. 1930

The Great Northern Hospital moved from Caledonian Road in 1884 to become the Royal Northern in Upper Holloway. In 1892 the first public baths to be established in Islington were bult on the old hospital site, with first and second class swimming baths and private baths (the picture shows Pool No. 2). In the first year 124,556 swimmers attended. The baths were demolished and rebuilt in 1980.

RICHMOND CRESCENT, c. 1900

Richmond Crescent was built in 1854, in the development of Sir George Thornhill's estate.

ARUNDEL SQUARE, c. 1910

The square was built in 1850. The public gardens and children's playground were set up in 1957.

CALEDONIAN ROAD, c. 1905

The Underground station was built in 1906 by the Great Northern, Piccadilly and Brompton Railway, now known simply as the Piccadilly line. The police station was built in 1856 (rebuilt in 1913, after this photograph was taken) on land bought from Samuel Pocock, whose name is remembered by the Pocock Arms next door. In the distance, on the corner of Hillmarton Road, is the Caledonian Road Wesleyan Chapel. It closed as a chapel in 1916 and was used as a warehouse until 1926 when it was reconsecrated as St. Mary's Liberal Catholic Church. In 1976 it became a clothing factory, and was demolished in 1983 to make way for housing.

MONEY ORDER DEPARTMENT, MANOR GARDENS, c. 1930

Manor Gardens took its name from a former moated farm house, known as Manor Farm, on Holloway Road near the end of Mercers Road. The large building in the centre of the picture is the Money Order Department, built by the GPO about 1910. The North branch of Islington Libraries was opened in 1906, the first public library in Islington. During World War I it was used as an annexe by the Royal Northern Hospital to treat wounded soldiers.

FOSTER'S BOOT REPAIRS, 34 GROVE ROAD, 1906

Charles Foster stands proudly at the door of the boot-shop in Grove Road (now Tollington Way), on the corner of Ingleby Road, an established business which he took over in 1906, and traded until 1912. Note the advertisement for the coming attractions at the Marlborough Theatre, built on Holloway Road in 1903 where now stands Marlborough House.

WOOD'S CHAPEL, HOLLOWAY ROAD, c. 1907

Upper Holloway Baptist Chapel, to give it the correct name, on the corner of Holloway Road and Tollington Way, was built in 1866–68. The minister from 1873 to 1911 was the Rev. J.R. Wood who was also President of the Baptist Union. The main roof collapsed in 1977, and the whole building was demolished in 1989. A new building has just (1991) been completed.

THE MARLBOROUGH TAVERN, HOLLOWAY ROAD, 1920–1930

Whereas Islington south of the Nag's Head developed mainly in the late 18th and early 19th centuries, Upper Holloway was built up in the later part of the 19th century. The Marlborough Tavern probably dates from about 1870, when building began in Marlborough Road.

MARLBOROUGH ROAD, c. 1910

Marlborough Road was built in 1867–69. This view is taken from the corner of Sussex Way (formerly Cottenham Road) looking towards Hornsey Road. The building with a gabled roof is a Mission Hall run by St. Mary's Church, Ashley Road.

DAVIES' DAIRY, c. 1910

The Davies Brothers opened their dairy at 150 Marlborough Road about 1910. Under various changes of ownership it continued as a dairy until 1970.

HOLLOWAY ROAD, c. 1910

This view looks from St. John's Villas to Fairbridge Road. Next to the hosier's shop was Thomson Brothers, pawnbrokers, and Henry Bennett the tailor. Herbert Tice had two shops, one a tobacconist and one a stationer, followed by Clement Edwards the butcher.

NEW COURT CONGREGATIONAL CHURCH, c. 1920

This is so named because it was built in Tollington Park in 1871 by worshippers who had been displaced from New Court, Lincoln's Inn Fields, where their chapel was demolished to facilitate the building of the Law Courts. It was sold to St. Mellitus Roman Catholic Church in 1959.

THE CORDWAINERS ARMS, ELTHORNE ROAD, c. 1920

This beer shop, on the corner of Ashbrook Road, was probably built in the 1880s. Edward George Mundy, the licensee during the 1920s, stands proudly at the door, flanked by his wife and some of his regular customers. The Cordwainers Arms gained a full pub licence in 1952, and was demolished in 1974 when this part of Elthorne Road was rebuilt.

ST. MARY'S CHURCH, ASHLEY ROAD, c. 1910

This church was built in 1860–61, when Ashley Road itself was being built. Its district was extended in 1983 to include that of the demolished St. Stephen, Elthorne Road.

CHEVERTON ROAD, c. 1910

Cheverton Road was built in 1874, and is named after Benjamin Cheverton (1794–1876), inventor, sculptor and adviser on the production of the first adhesive postage stamps, who lived in nearby Cornwallis Road. Note the milk delivery in cans.

FUNERAL PROCESSION OF DRIVER LUXTON, 15th June, 1912

Albert Roy Luxton was instructing a learner driver on an omnibus coming down Highgate Hill on Saturday the 8th of June 1912. They intended to turn into Hornsey Lane, but a wedding procession blocked the road. Because of the traffic congestion Luxton took over the wheel from the learner and decided to continue down Highgate Hill. The brakes failed at this point and Luxton steered the bus at a lamp standard to bring it to a halt, rather than risk other lives by letting it continue out of control down Holloway Road. He was taken by a passing tram to the Royal Northern Hospital where he died next day. He was 36 years old.

ALBERT LUXTON'S FUNERAL, 1912

The funeral procession on the 15th June went from his home in St. John's Way, along Holloway Road, Tufnell Park Road and Dartmouth Park Hill to Highgate Cemetery. The Holloway Town Silver Band played the Dead March, and hundreds of people lined the streets. A London General bus, draped in purple and black, bearing wreaths from many bus depots, followed the hearse. Fellow drivers in white coats formed an escort for the coffin at the cemetery.

VICTORIA ROAD, c. 1910

Victoria Road is in Haringey, just over the border from Islington, and runs from Upper Tollington Park to Stapleton Hall Road. The small spire in the distance is a Baptist chapel.

MOUNT PLEASANT VILLAS, c. 1905

This tree-lined road, built in the 1880s, is also in Haringey, and runs from Stapleton Hall Road to Mountview Road. The bridge carried the Edgware and Highgate line of the Great Northern railway. The railway no longer runs, and a nature trail named Parkland Walk now follows its line from Finsbury Park to Highgate Woods, and on to Alexandra Palace.

BAKERS' AND SWEEPS' FOOTBALL MATCH, c. 1910

About 1890 the Bakers and Sweeps of Islington formed themselves into a charity to give a Christmas dinner to the poor of the parish, and they were still going strong over twenty years later. They organised concerts to raise funds, and every Boxing Day they played a football match, the gate money being donated to the poor. The playing field is probably the Tufnell Park Football Club ground on Campdale Road.

TUFNELL PARK HOTEL, c. 1905

This pub is on the corner of Tufnell Park Road and Campdale Road. Tufnell Park Road dates from 1824, but most of the houses were built between 1850 and 1870. The Tufnell Park Hotel as shown no longer exists. It fell victim to a bomb in 1940 and was rebuilt as the Tufnell Park Tavern.

ST. GEORGE'S AVENUE, c. 1905

This photograph is wrongly titled. We are in Carleton Road, leading up to Tufnell Park Road. St. George's Avenue is to the left and its nameboard can just be seen. The octagonal building is St. George's Church, built in 1866–67, the design based on the church of St. George in Salonika. It had a detached tower and spire which is visible above the roofs of the houses. It closed for repair in 1963, but was vandalised and never re-opened as a church. It was converted into a theatre in 1976. A new church dedicated to St. George was built at the junction of Crayford and Carleton Roads in 1975.

DALMENY AVENUE, c. 1905

Dalmeny Avenue dates from 1863 and was first named St. Bartholomew Road. Blocks of flats replaced most of the houses in the years following the war.

DALMENY AVENUE, c. 1905

Ada Lewis House, a hostel for single women, was built in Dalmeny Avenue in 1945. Ada Travers Lewis, who died in 1931, was a pioneer of hostels for lone women in England and France.

CRAYFORD ROAD, c. 1905

As built in 1876–80, Crayford Road ran from Carleton Road to Parkhurst Road, but the south end of the street, from about the point where this photograph was taken, no longer exists. The two turnings to the right are, respectively, Cardwell and Tabley Roads.

TABLEY ROAD, c. 1905

Tabley Road was built in 1881. The baker's delivery van seems to have been momentarily abandoned whilst its driver comes forward to feature in the photograph.

YERBURY ROAD, c. 1905

Yerbury Road dates from about 1870, and was originally named as part of Mercers Road; it took its present name in 1877. This view looks from the corner of Rupert Road (on the immediate left) to where, at the bend of the road, Wedmore Street crosses. The children loitering outside the corner shop are leaning against a street fire alarm.

HUGO ROAD, c. 1905
Hugo Road was built in 1887.

JUNCTION ROAD STATION, c. 1910

In 1870 the Midland Railway started running suburban trains between Moorgate Street and Crouch Hill. In 1872 a station was opened on Junction Road where the road crosses over the railway near Wyndham Crescent. In 1916 it ceased to be a passenger station, and was used only for cattle, coal and goods. It closed in 1960.

ISLINGTON BOROUGH COUNCIL CART No. 149

It is difficult to date this picture, but it must be after 1900, the year when Islington became a Borough Council. Electric lorries were introduced for dust-bin collection in 1921, but horse-drawn carts still continued in use for some years.

ACKNOWLEDGEMENTS

The postcards reproduced in this book are all from the collection of Dick Whetstone who has spent many years patiently searching out these rare pictures. To those of us who like to look back to the past, historical photographs are a delight, and we are fortunate in having Dick Whetstone as one of Islington's citizens.

Our thanks are gratefully given to the Borough Librarian and the staff of Islington Reference Libraries for allowing access to their Archive Collection, which is of inestimable value to the local historian; and to the Guildhall Library.